Off to School We Go!

by Laura Vey

Illustrated by Darryl Ligasan

PEARSON

Glenview, Illinois • Boston, Massachusetts • Chandler, Arizona
Upper Saddle River, New Jersey

buildings

city

Matt lives in the city.
Matt and Dad walk to school.
They see many buildings.

Emma lives in the country.
She walks to school with her friend.
They see many fields.

fields

country

sign

Matt sees a sign.
The sign means "walk."

Emma sees a truck.
The driver says, "Please cross."

driver

truck

Matt sees a hat in a store.
"I like that hat," says Matt.

Emma sees a pumpkin in a field.
"I like that pumpkin," says Emma.

pumpkin

field

Matt lives in the city. Matt sees buildings.

Emma lives in the country. Emma sees fields.

What do you see?